First HARP BOOK

BY

Betty Paret

Ed. 1725

G. SCHIRMER, Inc.

DISTRIBUTED BY

 HAL•LEONARD®
CORPORATION
7777 W. BLUEMOUND RD. P.O. BOX 13819 MILWAUKEE, WI 53213

PREFACE

This book is NOT a "Method".

It is a book of carefully graded material which ANY teacher may use in giving a pedagogically sound and fundamentally thorough approach to playing the harp.

39641

CONTENTS

First Harp Book

Betty Paret

Copy-Cat

Waltz

Lis - ten to the big church bell: Ding, dong, ding, dong, ding, dong, bell.

Alphabet Song

French Traditional Tune
attributed to N. Dezède (1744-1792)

A B C D E F G, H I J K L M N O P;

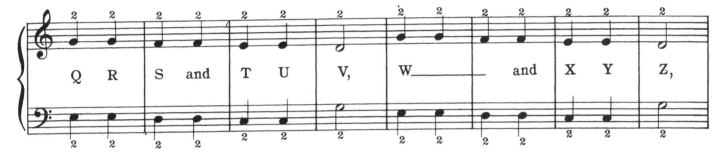

Q R S and T U V, W_____ and X Y Z,

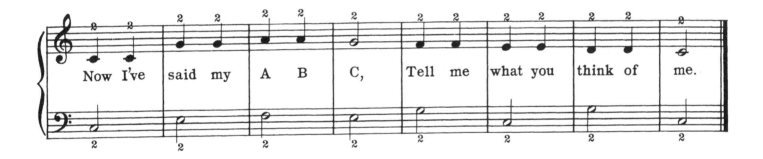

Now I've said my A B C, Tell me what you think of me.

Swinging

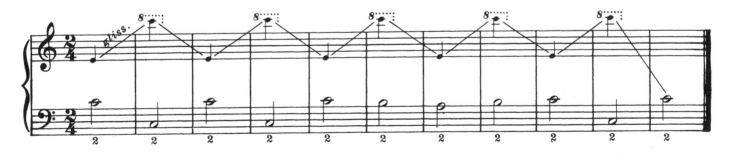

Exercises for Two Fingers of the Right Hand

The diamond-shaped note ◊ represents the string to be held.

Exercises for Two Fingers of the Left Hand

Jumping

Wooden-Shoe Dance

Breton Folk-Song

Lively

Danc-ing, Danc-ing, gai-ly danc-ing! Danc-ing, in my wood-en shoes.

Cuckoo

German Folk-Song

Cuck-oo, Cuck-oo sings in the wood. Springtime is com-ing;

Flow-ers are bloom-ing. Cuck-oo, Cuck-oo sings in the wood.

Rocking

Not too fast

Connect all the notes in the right hand

l. h.

Russian Tune

Slowly

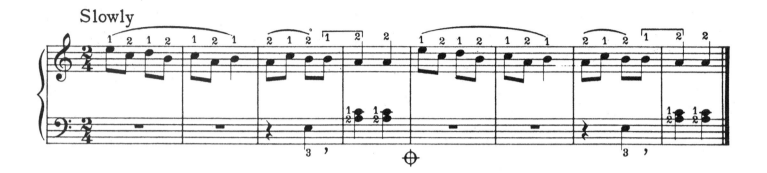

Star Dance

Pawnee Indian Tune

Strong and steady

Fix E♯

Left hand very soft to imitate a tom-tom

Exercises for Three Fingers of the Right Hand

Exercises for Three Fingers of the Left Hand

Scale Snippets

With rhythmic swing

French Folk-Tune

10

Sur le Pont d'Avignon

French Folk-Song

Long, Long Ago

Thomas H. Bayly

9641

Pussy Cat

Nursery Rhyme

Pus-sy Cat, Pus-sy Cat, where have you been? I've been to Lon-don to vis-it the Queen.

Folk-Song

Swedish

Gaily

Swedish Folk-Dance

Lively

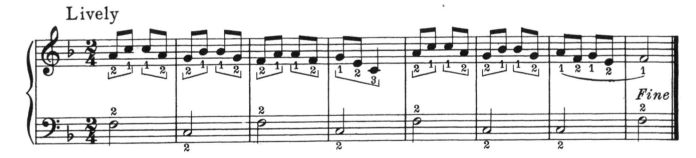

The Jolly Peasant

Bohemian Folk-Dance

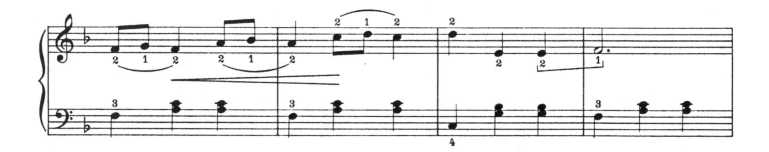

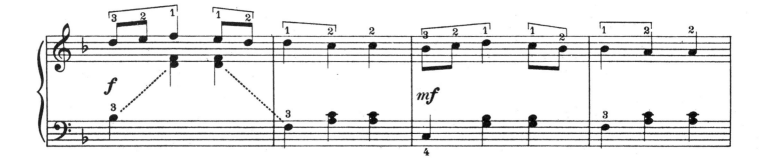

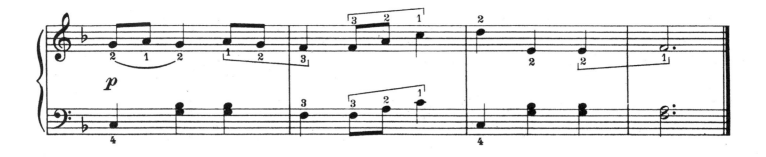

Rondo

Betty Paret

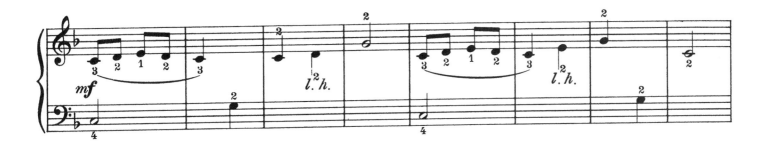

39641

Exercises for Four Fingers of the Right Hand

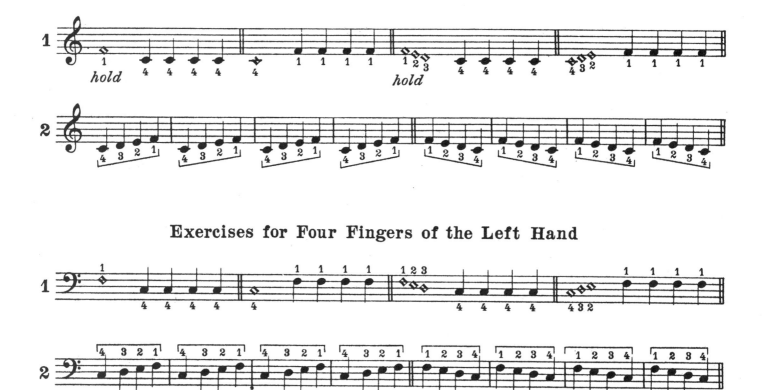

Exercises for Four Fingers of the Left Hand

Rain Song

Bohemian Folk-Song

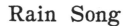

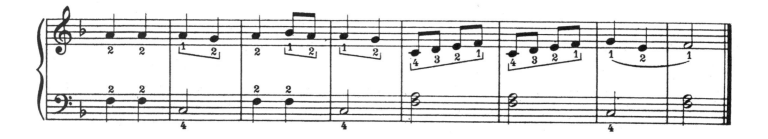

Lavender's Blue

English Folk-Song

Scale Game

For Sharp Keys

C D E F G A B C, C B A G F E D C. Next we have the Key of G:

G A B C D E F♯ G, G F♯ E D C B A G. Next we have the Key of D.

This may be continued throughout all the sharp keys.

For Flat Keys

C D E F G A B C C B A G F E D C. New key of F: F G A B♭ C D E F,

This may be continued throughout all the flat keys.

The Keys of Heaven

I'll give you the keys of heav'n,
I'll give you the keys of heav'n,
Madam, will you walk?
Madam, will you talk?
Madam, will you walk and talk with me?

English Folk-Song

Moderately

En Roulant

Gaily

French-Canadian Singing-Game

Lota

Swedish Folk-Tune

Barbara Allen

In Scarlet Town, where I was born,
There was a fair maid dwelling,
Made every youth cry "Well-a-day!"
Her name was Barbara Allen.

English Ballad

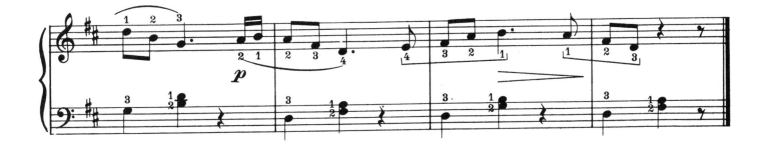

Study in Intervals

2nd   3rd   4th   5th   6th   7th   octave

Interval Exercises

Repeat all in the left hand. Later do all with two hands at once.

Break all the above intervals into the following patterns.

Night Song

Slavonic Folk-Song

Slowly

Shepherd's Cradle-Song

Swedish Folk-Tune

Very slowly

The Bluebells of Scotland

Oh where, tell me where, is your Highland laddie gone?
Oh where, tell me where, is your Highland laddie gone?
He's gone to fight the foe for King George upon the throne
And it's oh, in my heart, how I wish him safe at home.

Scottish Folk-Song

Not too fast

A Riddle

A tiny man I see standing in the wood;
He wears upon his head a purple hood.
Guess who can this wee man be,
Standing there so silently
In the deep, dark shadows of the wood?

German Folk-Song

Moderately

The Wonderful Inn

German Folk-Song

Le Bon Petit Roi d'Yvetot

Il était un roi d'Yvetot
Peu connu dans l'histoire,
Se levant tard, se couchant tôt,
Dormant fort bien sans gloire,
Et couronné par Jeanneton
D'un simple bonnet de coton.
Oh! Oh! Oh! Oh! Ah! Ah! Ah! Ah!
Quel bon petit roi c'était là!

Il faisait ses quatre repas
Dans son palais de chaume,
Et sur un âne, pas à pas,
Parcourait son royaume,
Joyeux, simple et croyant le bien,
Pour toute garde il n'avait rien qu'un chien.
Oh! Oh! Oh! Oh! Ah! Ah! Ah! Ah!
Quel bon petit roi c'était là!

The little king of Yvetot
In history was unknown.
He got up late, slept well at night
Because he had no throne,
And on his head wore for a crown
A cotton bonnet like his gown.
Ah! Ah! Ah! Ah! Oh! Oh! Oh! Oh!
Good little king of Yvetot.

Within his castle warm and bright
His feasts were very grand,
And on his donkey step by step
He went through all the land.
His little dog would trot behind
To guard this king so good and kind.
Ah! Ah! Ah! Ah! Oh! Oh! Oh! Oh!
Good little king of Yvetot.

—*English version by Betty Paret*

French Folk-Song

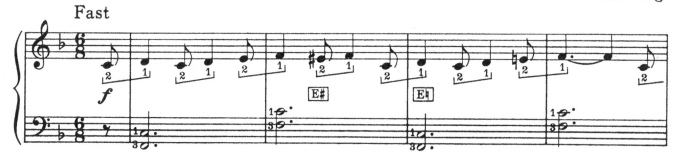

Note: On an Irish harp the E♯ may be played as F.

The Keel Row

As I came thro' Sandgate,
Thro' Sandgate, thro' Sandgate,
As I came thro' Sandgate,
I heard a lassie sing:
"Oh, weel may the keel row,
The keel row, the keel row,
Weel may the keel row
That my laddie's in."

"He wears a blue bonnet,
Blue bonnet, blue bonnet,
He wears a blue bonnet,
A dimple in his chin."
"Oh, weel may the keel row,
The keel row, the keel row,
Weel may the keel row
That my laddie's in."

Scottish Folk-Song

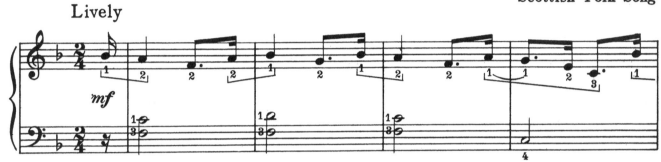

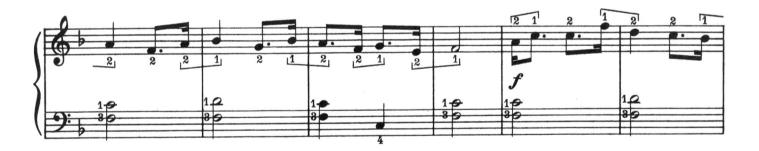

The Judge's Dance

Swedish

Chord Exercises for the Right Hand (Three Fingers)

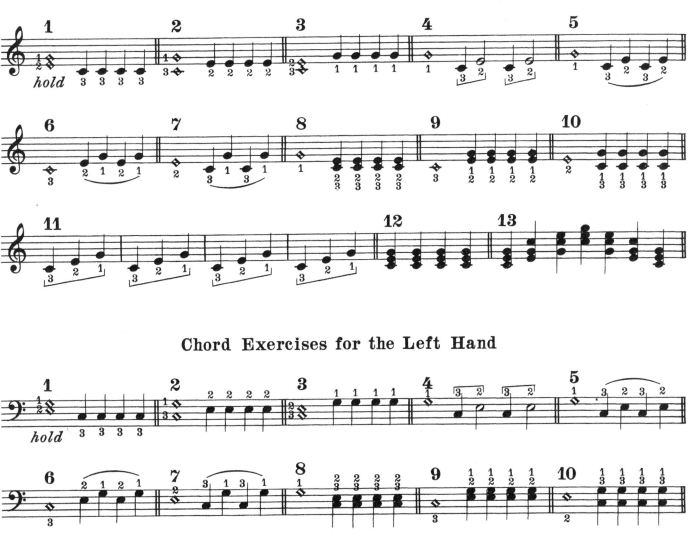

Chord Exercises for the Left Hand

These exercises may be applied to any three-finger chord.

Song of the Evening Bell

Hymn of Thanksgiving

We gather together to ask the Lord's blessing,
He chastens and hastens His will to make known.
The wicked oppressing cease them from distressing,
Sing praises to His name, He forgets not His own.
—Translated by Theodore Baker

Netherlands Tune

Slowly

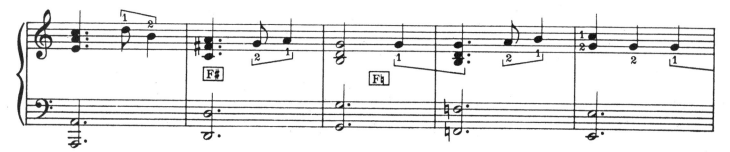

Jardin d'Amour

Slowly and gracefully

Old French Waltz

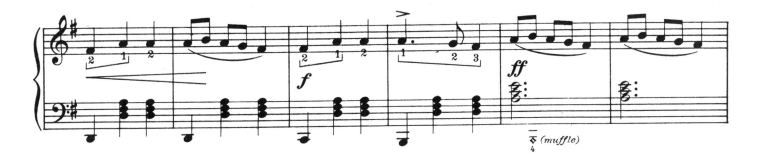

O'Carolan's* Air

Moderately

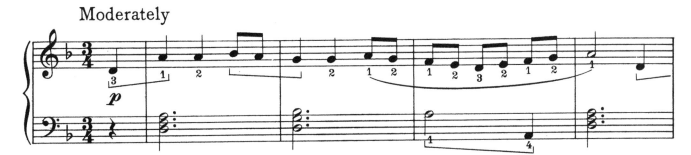

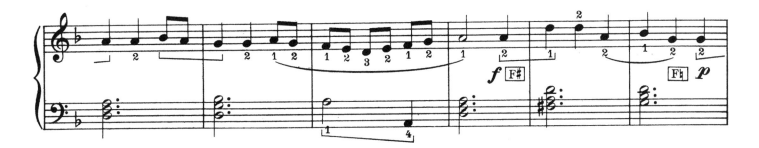

*O'Carolan was a blind Irish harper of the 17th century.

39641

Andante
from the "Surprise" Symphony

Josef Haydn

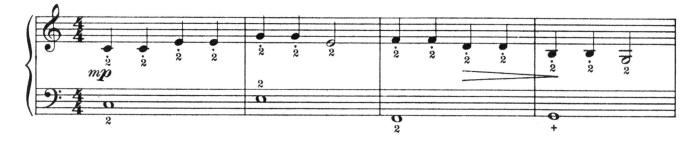

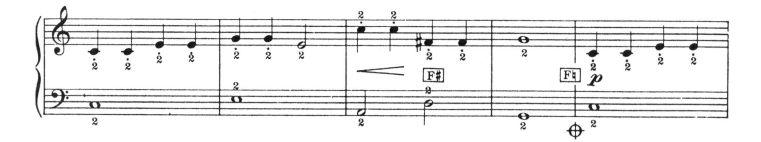

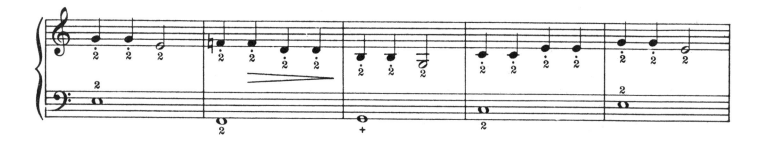

Waltz

Franz Schubert, Op. 77, No. 2

Gracefully

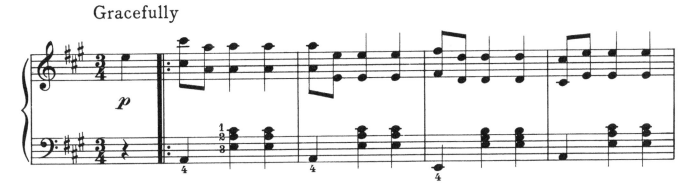

The Foggy Dew

Irish Folk-Tune

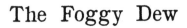

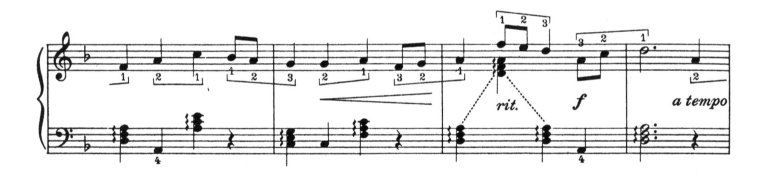

Leezie Lindsay

1.
Will ye gang to the Hielands, Leezie Lindsay?
Will ye gang to the Hielands wi' me?
Will ye gang to the Hielands, Leezie Lindsay?
My bride and my darling to be.

2.
To gang to the Hielands wi' you, Sir,
I dinna ken how that may be;
For I ken na the road I am gaeing,
Nor ken I the lad I'm gaun wi'!

3.
O Leezie Lindsay lass, ye maun ken little,
For sae ye be dinna ken me;
For my name is Lord Ronald MacDonald,
A chieftain o' high degree.

4.
She has gotten a gown o' green satin,
She has kilted it up to the knee;
And she's off wi' Lord Ronald MacDonald,
His bride and his darling to be.

Scottish Folk-Song

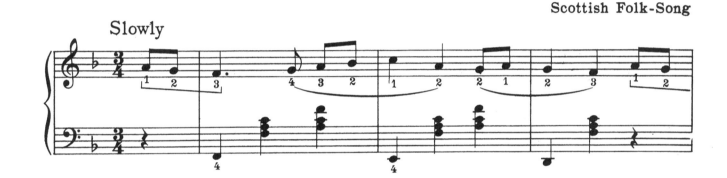

Chord Exercises for the Right Hand (Four Fingers)

Chord Exercises for the Left Hand

Drink to Me Only

Drink to me only with thine eyes,
   And I will pledge with mine;
Or leave a kiss but in the cup
   And I'll not look for wine.
The thirst that from the soul doth rise
   Doth ask a drink divine;
But might I of Jove's nectar sup,
   I would not change for thine.

                —Ben Jonson

English Tune

All through the Night

Welsh Folk-Song

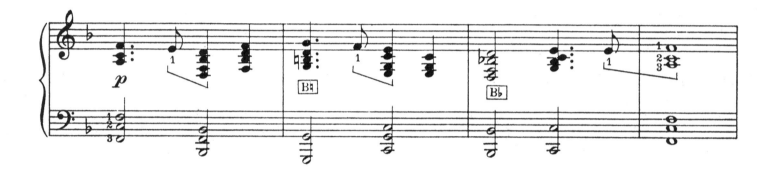

German Dance

Franz Schubert, Op. 33, No. 7

Slowly and calmly

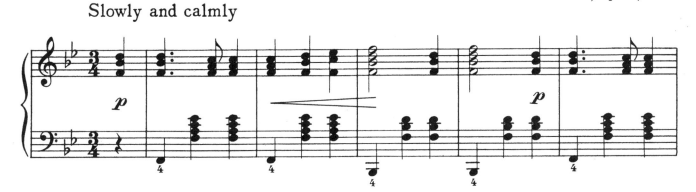

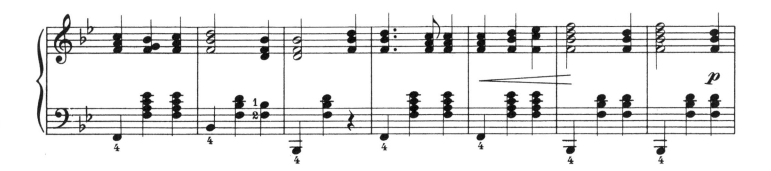

Flowers in the Valley

1.

O there was a woman and she was a widow,
Fair are the flow'rs in the valley,
With a daughter as fair as a fresh sunny meadow,
The Red, the Green, and the Yellow,
The Harp, the Lute, the Pipe, the Flute, the Cymbal,
Sweet goes the treble Violin.
The maid so rare and the flow'rs so fair,
Together they grew in the valley.

2.

There came a Knight all clothed in red,
Fair are the flow'rs in the valley,
"I would thou wert my bride," he said,
The Red, the Green, and the Yellow,
The Harp, the Lute, the Pipe, the Flute, the Cymbal,
Sweet goes the treble Violin.
"I would," she sighed, "Ne'er wins a bride!"
Fair are the flow'rs in the valley.

3.

There came a Knight all clothed in green,
Fair are the flow'rs in the valley,
"This maid so sweet might be my queen",
The Red, the Green, and the Yellow,
The Harp, the Lute, the Pipe, the Flute, the Cymbal,
Sweet goes the treble Violin.
"Might be," sighed she, "Will ne'er win me!"
Fair are the flow'rs in the valley.

4.

There came a Knight, in yellow was he,
Fair are the flow'rs in the valley,
"My bride, my queen, thou must with me!"
The Red, the Green, and the Yellow,
The Harp, the Lute, the Pipe, the Flute, the Cymbal,
Sweet goes the treble Violin.
With blushes red, "I come," she said;
"Farewell to the flow'rs in the valley".

Not too fast

English Folk-Song

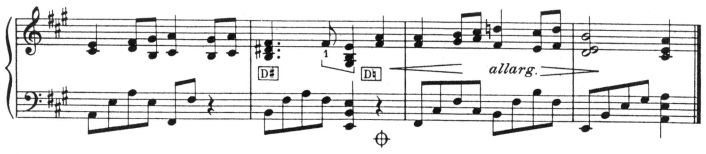

Wi' a Hundred Pipers

Wi' a hundred pipers an' a', an' a',
Wi' a hundred pipers an' a', an' a',
We'll up an' gie them a blaw, a blaw,
Wi' a hundred pipers an' a', an' a',
Oh, it's owre the Border, awa', awa',
It's owre the Border, awa', awa',
We'll on and we'll march to Carlisle ha',
Wi' its yetts, its castle, an' a', an' a',
Wi' a hundred pipers an' a', an' a',
Wi' a hundred pipers an' a', an' a',
We'll up an' gie them a blaw, a blaw,
Wi' a hundred pipers an' a', an' a',

Scottish Air

Moderately

Note: On an Irish harp the E♯ may be played as F.

39641